THE FAMILY BLESSING

Discover the powerful gift of legacy and life God has given you through your words

ROLF GARBORG

Unless otherwise specified, all Scripture quotations are taken from *The Everyday Bible, New Century Version.* Copyright © 1987, 1988 by Word Publishing, Dallas, Texas 75039. Used by permission.

Scripture quotations marked (KJV) are taken from the *King James Version* of the Bible.

Scripture quotations marked (NKJV) are taken from *The New King James Version.* Copyright © 1979, 1980, 1982, Thomas Nelson, Inc.

Scripture quotations marked (NAS) are taken from the *New American Standard Bible.* Copyright © the Lockman Foundation 1960, 1962, 1963, 1968, 1971, 1972, 1973, 1975, 1977. Used by permission.

Scripture quotations marked (NIV) are taken from *The Holy Bible: New International Version®.* NIV®. Copyright © 1973, 1978, 1984 by International Bible Society. Used by permission of Zondervan Publishing House. All rights reserved.

Author emphasis in Scripture quotations is in italics.

12 11 10 09 08 07   10 9 8 7 6 5 4 3 2 1

The Family Blessing—
Discover the powerful gift of legacy and life God has given you through your words
ISBN 1-59379-120-8 (Formerly ISBN 1-57794-435-6 & 1-59379-004-X)

4090 154th Street
Prior Lake, MN 55372

Published by White Stone Books
P.O. Box 2835
Lakeland, Florida 33806

TO MARY,

my precious wife of more than thirty years,

my most ardent friend, encourager,

counselor, and companion,

and mother of my two most

cherished gifts from God,

Carlton and Lisa.

CONTENTS

PREFACE

If it's good, God did it. And if it's bad,
I did it, and it's worse than it looks.
A. W. TOZER

Tozer's statement rings incredibly true. It seems as if every time I began to look admiringly at something I had done well and taken credit for, God allowed something to happen that would correct my thinking.

Sometimes correction would come through direct confrontation from a friend honest enough to tell me the truth about myself; sometimes a subtle, sarcastic remark from an acquaintance would do the job. And sometimes it was just the hollow, empty feeling I would get when I took undeserving credit. *The Family Blessing* is a clear example of Tozer's principle. I know that the practice of blessing the family is good; it is a gift from God. Also, I know that in pronouncing the blessing, we are the instruments God uses, the vessels through whom He flows. And because God's gifts are meant to be shared, I'm offering this book.

In no way do I mean to communicate that all has gone smoothly. As a family we have had our share of failures, setbacks, problems, and disappointments. Only God's grace has made it work, and I'm grateful that He is still at work in us.

Over the years, I've shared the practice of blessing our children with other families. The responses have almost always been the same:

1. "I wish I had known this when my kids were young."
2. "I wish my parents had done that for me." (This comment came mostly from teenagers.)
3. "How do I start?"
4. "What blessings do you use, and where do you find them?"
5. "You should write a book about this."

Here then is the book to help you learn about blessing and how to make it a part of your life. It suggests blessings to use and offers insights into what blessing your family can mean to you, regardless of your childhood or the age of your children. It's never too late to bless and be blessed.

God bless you as you read!

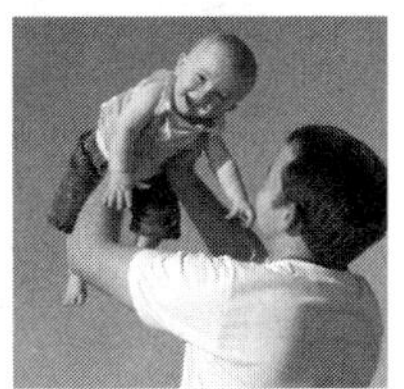

THE LORD BLESS YOU, AND KEEP YOU;

The Lord make His face shine on you,

And be gracious to you;

The Lord lift up His countenance on you,

And give you peace.

NUMBERS 6:24-26 NAS

CHAPTER ONE

BLESSING BEGINNINGS

The Lord bless you, and keep you.

I still remember the scene: It was a balmy January evening in San Juan, Puerto Rico, in 1972. The nighttime street noises came freely through the open louvered window of the bedroom as my young son, Carlton, lay sound asleep.

I don't remember how long I simply stood by his bed that night, thinking about what a treasure he was. So many times before Carlton was born I had watched fathers with their young children. Now that I had a son who was nearly three years old, I wanted so desperately to be a good father to him.

Carlton didn't stir when I sat on the edge of his bed. As I leaned over his little body, I thought, *Lord Jesus, You showed us how much You care for these little ones when You took them in Your arms and blessed them. Now I want to do the same for my child. Take this blessing of mine and use it for Your glory.* Then I placed my hand gently on his head and whispered into his ear a blessing I had heard so many times in church, adding to it his name:

Take this blessing of mine and use it for Your glory.

The Lord bless you, Carlton, and keep you.
The Lord make His face shine upon you and
be gracious unto you;
The Lord lift up His countenance upon you
and give you peace.
In the name of the Father, and of the Son,
and of the Holy Spirit. Amen.

It seemed so natural—so right. I felt as if I had obeyed God by doing this.

Before I rose to leave Carlton's room, I kissed him on the cheek, told him I loved him, and wiped the remaining tears from my face. Then I lingered there in the darkness and breathed a prayer of thanks to God for giving us this gift of a son and for blessing him. Little did I realize that the scene would be repeated thousands of times in the years to come.

That was the first night I gave my son a blessing. The idea was new to me, and I didn't fully understand what it was about. But after talking with another Christian father who gave his children a blessing every night, I had become convinced that this simple practice could transform our children's lives.

This simple practice could transform our children's lives.

That year a recently released best-seller caught my eye: *The Christian Family* by Larry Christenson.[1] In it the author, who at the time was the pastor of a Lutheran church in San Pedro, California, clearly and biblically showed us God's order for the family and how we can practice the presence of Jesus in the home. I was immediately taken by the simplicity of the message in this book and began to recommend it to others.

When an opportunity came to invite Larry to Puerto Rico, I gladly took advantage of it. He agreed to come and spend a week at our mission, teaching and sharing with us. One evening I asked Larry about a section in his book that dealt with the Christensens' practice of speaking a blessing on their children individually as they put them to bed each night. He said that he and his wife, Nordis, had been living in West Germany with their four young children when they first heard of the idea. It was a custom that was practiced by a couple they had met, Hans-Jochen Arp and his wife, Elisabeth.

Hans-Jochen told them how he would speak a blessing on each of his six children as they went to bed. Even if they were already asleep when he came home late, he would go into their bedrooms and bless them.

Larry and Nordis were so impressed with the idea that they went home that very night to bless their own children. First, they explained to them what they were doing and why. With four children, it took awhile to give everyone an individual blessing. But they did and continued to do it faithfully until each child was grown. Now Larry was sharing the idea with others.

The idea made sense. After all, we knew that many pastors bless their congregations at the end of each Sunday church service. Often they hold out their hands toward the people in a symbolic gesture of covering and then recite a benediction from the words of Scripture, such as the one the high priest Aaron spoke over the ancient Israelites:

The Lord bless you and keep you:
the Lord make His face shine upon you,
and be gracious unto you;
the Lord lift up His countenance upon you,
and give you peace.

NUMBERS 6:24-26[2]

Then they may add words, such as: "In the name of the Father, and of the Son, and of the Holy Spirit. Amen."

Just as the pastor of a congregation has an opportunity to bless, we realized that parents as priests in their households have a similar privilege. They can speak at home the kind of blessing pastors speak to their churches.

As we talked with Larry on into the night, I became convinced that this family practice was right for us as well. What I didn't realize back then was how many benefits could come from making this commitment to bless my children.

So I made a decision. Whenever and however possible, I would bless my child every day. And I would begin that night.

After I'd given Carlton a blessing that evening, Mary and I agreed together to commit to this practice every night as we tucked him into bed. I could hardly wait for the next night to come so I could do it again, this time with Carlton awake.

During our discussion, I had already begun thinking of how it would be to have two kids to bless each night. As we continued talking, the realization came to me: We weren't done with the blessing this evening. I already *had* two children. Mary was just three months away from giving birth to our second child. Why not start now to bless them both? So I reached out my hand, placed it on Mary's stomach, and said, "Lord, I don't have any idea who it is You have for us in here, but I commit this gift of a child to You." Then, speaking to that unborn baby with my hand still on Mary, I spoke the blessing, just as I had with Carlton.

On April 23, 1972, Lisa Faith Garborg entered this world "sunny-side up," and she hasn't quit smiling yet. No doubt one reason for her joy is that she has been blessed every day by her fathers—both earthly and heavenly—since even before she was born.

Carlton and Lisa are now adults with children of their own, and amazingly enough, both of them still check in nearly every day to receive their blessing. My children's desire to continue receiving our daily blessing is just one indication of the impact it has made on their lives and on the lives of their children as they pass the blessing on. I know that the family blessing is much more than a bedtime ritual.

Let's look at the significance of the blessing from a biblical standpoint to discover why it can become such a meaningful part of the fabric of your daily family life.

BLESSED SHALL YOU BE IN THE CITY,

and blessed shall you be in the country.

Blessed shall be the offspring of your body and the

produce of your ground and the offspring of your beasts,

the increase of your herd and the young of your flock.

Blessed shall be your basket and your kneading bowl.

Blessed shall you be when you come in,

and blessed shall you be when you go out.

DEUTERONOMY 28:3-6 NAS

CHAPTER TWO

THE BIBLICAL BLESSING

When God launched Abraham onto a course that would fulfill his destiny, He sent him from his parents' home into unknown territory. No doubt Abraham's excitement over his future was mixed with considerable apprehension over what lay ahead—the same kind of apprehension most of us felt when we first launched out on our own, leaving our parents' home forever.

How did God choose to prepare Abraham for the days ahead and to encourage him along the way? He provided a *blessing:*

I will make you into a great nation and I will bless you;
I will make your name great, and you will be a blessing.
I will bless those who bless you, and whoever curses you
I will curse;
and all peoples on earth will be blessed through you.

GENESIS 12:2,3 NIV

With these words the Lord spoke to Abraham a blessing of greatness, promised further blessing in the future, and said He would make the man a blessing to others—even a channel of blessing to the entire world. No doubt in the years to come, whenever Abraham faced challenges, these words from God strengthened and sustained him.

The God of Abraham was a God of blessing.

Throughout the Bible we find ample evidence that the God of Abraham was a God of blessing. In fact, the words *bless* or *blessing* appear in Scripture in some form or another about seven hundred times. Apparently Abraham, along with countless other people in the Bible, needed and welcomed the grace, power, and encouragement that could be poured into their lives through God's blessing.

But what is a blessing? The word has a variety of meanings in modern English, so let's look at two ancient biblical words to define what is meant by the term.

The Old Testament Hebrew word for blessing is *berakah.* To the ancient Hebrews, a *berakah* was the transmittal or endowment of the power of God's goodness and favor, usually through the spoken word and often with the accompanying act of the laying on of hands.[1] For Abraham, the *berakah* was God's spoken declaration of favor that would convey God's power to make him into a great nation and able to transmit that divine favor and power to the whole world.

The Hebrews believed that the spoken word carried great power for good or evil. Most ancient peoples were convinced, as the Hebrews were, that words once spoken take a life of their own. So when a word of blessing was given, the speaker could not retract it.

When a word of blessing was given, the speaker could not retract it.

That was the case with Isaac's blessing, which was given mistakenly to his younger son, Jacob, rather than to his firstborn, Esau. (Gen. 27:1-40.) In this Bible story, we read that Jacob tricked his blind father into thinking he was Esau, so Isaac placed his hands on Jacob and pronounced on him the blessing of the firstborn child that rightfully belonged to Esau. Once Isaac spoke the words, there was nothing he could do to take back the blessing, even though it had been gained by deceit. The most the saddened father could do was to speak another blessing on Esau.

Benedictions (spoken blessings) such as Isaac's were commonly spoken by fathers to their children. They were also given by people in authority to those under their authority, or by priests to the congregation. Such benedictions always included the name of God.

In the New Testament, the word most often translated as "bless" is the Greek verb *eulogeo,* from which we get the words *eulogy* and *eulogize.* It means literally "to speak well of" or "to praise."[2]

As in the Old Testament, this blessing was often the act of calling down God's gracious power on someone. One clear example of this act in the New Testament is when Jesus blessed the disciples just before He ascended to heaven by promising that God would send the gracious power of the Holy Spirit on them. (Luke 24:48-51.)

FOUR TYPES OF BLESSING

One way to better understand blessings for our present purposes is to make a distinction according to the giver and receiver of the blessing. Using this criteria, there are four types of blessing found in the Scripture.

1. A blessing *spoken by God to people*

This was a benediction by God, promising His favor, such as the blessing given to Abraham.

2. A blessing *spoken by people to God*

When we "speak well of" or "express praise" to God, then we're blessing Him, as David did: "*Bless* the Lord, O my soul, and forget none of His benefits" (Ps. 103:2 NAS). The apostle Paul echoed that sentiment when he wrote to the Ephesians, "*Blessed* be the God and Father of our Lord Jesus Christ, who has *blessed* us with every spiritual *blessing*" (Eph. 1:3 NKJV).

3. A blessing spoken by God or people over things

Deuteronomy 28 is filled with this kind of blessing. God promises to pour out His favor on the material resources of the Israelites if they obey Him: "*Blessed* shall be . . . the produce of your ground and the offspring of your beasts. . . . *Blessed* shall be your basket and your kneading bowl" (Deut. 28:4,5 NAS).

People also spoke blessings over things as a way of dedicating them to God and setting them apart for His favor. The most common example is the blessing of food, an ancient Jewish custom that continues in the Christian community. Jesus showed the great potential power of such a practice when He blessed the loaves and fishes, calling down God's miraculous power to multiply them. (Matt. 14:19-21.)

4. A blessing spoken by one person to another

This was done in the name of God, who is the source of all blessing. Isaac's blessing of Jacob is one example of this kind; Aaron's blessing on the Israelites is another.

In this last category, please note that the word *blessing* can have both a general and specific meaning. The general meaning can be referred to by the literal translation of *eulogeo:* "to speak well of, to express praise."

This is the sense probably intended when Jesus told His disciples, "*Bless* those who curse you, pray for those who mistreat you" (Luke 6:28 NIV). Thus, Paul was obeying the Lord's command when he replied to his persecutors with gracious speech: "When we are cursed, we bless . . . when we are slandered, we answer kindly" (1 Cor. 4:12,13 NIV).

The more specific meaning of blessing is the intentional act of speaking God's favor and power into someone's life, often accompanied by a gesture such as laying hands on the person. This is the kind of blessing spoken by Isaac to his son Jacob, and in turn by Jacob to his sons. (Gen. 48:8-49:28.) It's the type of blessing Jesus gave to His disciples (Luke 24:50) and to the children (Mark 10:16).

In *The Family Blessing* we will look at both the specific and the general meanings of blessing within the context of family life. When the power of the spoken word for good or evil in our daily conversations at home is recognized, we can learn to use that power intentionally to bring blessing to our children.

HOW BLESSED IS EVERYONE WHO FEARS THE LORD,

Who walks in His ways.
When you shall eat of the fruit of your hands,
You will be happy and it will be well with you.
Your wife shall be like a fruitful vine,
Within your house,
Your children like olive plants
Around your table.
Behold, for thus shall the man be blessed
Who fears the Lord.
The Lord bless you,
And may you see prosperity all the days of your life.
Indeed, may you see your children's children!
Peace be upon God's people!

ADAPTED FROM PSALM 128 NAS

CHAPTER THREE

BLESSING THE FAMILY

The Lord make His face shine on you.

The hit musical play and film *Fiddler on the Roof* has tugged at the heartstrings of thousands of parents with its charming story of love and conflict in family life. Many parents can identify with the hopes and fears, the convictions and questions of Jewish Papa Tevye and Mama Golde as they struggle to rear their children in a godly way and to help prepare them for happy and productive adult lives.

One of the most poignant scenes from the play shows the family at the table of the Sabbath meal. When all have gathered, they perform the ancient customs associated with that meal. The mother lights the Sabbath candles, prays, and then joins her husband in singing to the children "Sabbath Prayer," a simple song of blessing that expresses their desires:

May the Lord protect and defend you,
May He always shield you from shame;
May you come to be in Yisroel [Israel] a shining name.
May you be like Ruth and like Esther,
May you be deserving of praise;
Strengthen them, oh Lord, and keep them from the
stranger's ways.
May God bless you and grant you long lives,
May the Lord fulfill our Sabbath prayer for you.
May God make you good mothers and wives.
May He send you husbands who will care for you.
May the Lord protect and defend you,
May the Lord preserve you from pain;
Favor them, oh Lord, with happiness and peace,
Oh hear our Sabbath prayer. Amen.[1]

What Christian parent doesn't hear echoed in those words the deepest sentiments of his or her own heart? And yet how many of us have a regular setting where such powerful words can be expressed to our children?

Christian families can adopt the Jewish community's ancient tradition of parents' giving their children a benediction simply by personalizing this biblical custom according to their family's needs.

You may say or sing a blessing; you may express it daily, weekly, or on special occasions. You can select a Scripture to use or create your own blessing based on Scripture. However you choose to bless your children, the family blessing—acted out so beautifully on the stage in this play—can become a real-life scene in your own home. And it will confirm your children in godliness by speaking into their lives the grace of their heavenly Father.

OUR CHILDREN'S HIGHEST GOOD

When Jesus came to earth two thousand years ago, He came to accomplish one overwhelming task: to give Himself to our highest good, that we would know and love God with all our heart. Just read what He prayed to His Father in John 17:3-4: "And this is eternal life: that men can know you, the only true God, and that men can know Jesus Christ, the One you sent. I finished the work you gave me to do. I brought you glory on earth."

Jesus came to give Himself to our highest good.

Again in Luke 10:25-28, when Jesus was questioned by a teacher of the law on how to gain eternal life, He replied with a question: "What is written in the law?" The teacher answered, "Love the Lord your God. Love him with all your heart, all your soul, all your strength, and all your mind. And you must love your neighbor as you love yourself." Then Jesus said to him, "Your answer is right. Do this and you will have life forever."

The single most important concern we should have as parents should be the same primary concern Jesus has for us: *We must make it our ultimate goal to help our children know and love God with all their heart.*

How do we do that? One of the simplest and most powerful ways to help children know and love God is to give them a daily, concrete encounter with His power and favor by laying hands on them and speaking a blessing.

The concept of a parent speaking a blessing on a child may seem strange, but it is scriptural. It's an ancient and respected custom dating back to biblical times. In fact, the family setting for the blessing apparently predates its use in the public setting; the priest or other official who spoke benedictions on the people of Israel was only supplementing the most basic of blessings—the one given by the father to the children.

Even those who have never given or received this kind of blessing have probably caught glimpses of it in various contexts, such as benedictions in church services or the scene just described in *Fiddler on the Roof.* Several Old Testament stories focus on this custom, some of which were previously mentioned: Isaac's blessing of Jacob (Gen. 27); Jacob's blessing of his sons and grandsons (Gen. 48:8-49:33); the priest Melchizedek's blessing of Abram (Gen. 14:18-20); the high priest Aaron's blessing of the Israelites (Num. 6:23-27); and the prophet Balaam's blessing of the Israelites (Num. 23:7-24:9).

HOW WE USE THE BLESSING IN OUR HOME

In our family, the approach we used in blessing our children was quite simple.

Each evening at bedtime, I would lay my hands on the head of each of my children and speak the blessing that appears in Numbers 6:24-26, adding at the end the words "in the name of the Father, and of the Son, and of the Holy Spirit," and personalizing it to each child by including his or her name.

It was that simple. We just spoke the same blessing to our children each night. And they came to depend on it as a token of security and a sign of their parents' continuing love for them.

Of course, even though our blessing was simple, busy schedules seemed to conspire to complicate matters. A little flexibility helped us maintain the blessing in our household over the years.

In biblical times, certain people were considered to be endowed with a special authority to bless or to curse: priests, prophets, and fathers, for example. But a blessing could be given by anyone. This is especially important to know in establishing the blessing in your home today.

The primary role of blessing in our household has always rested on me as the husband and father. But because of work-related travel, I've not always been present to give the blessing.

Knowing that anyone can give this blessing relieved some of my concern about my travel schedule. When I was away from home, Mary assumed the responsibility of blessing the kids and often blessed them with me when I was home.

When I was away on business, I would call home as often as possible. After catching up on the day's events with both children, I would bless them individually over the phone.

Frequently, if the kids thought I was going to forget, or if they had to leave, they would say, "Dad, can I have my blessing now?" They wouldn't miss it for any reason, and their commitment to the practice helped assure that the family blessing was a permanent fixture in our home.

JESUS BLESSED THE CHILDREN

When Jesus walked here on earth, He was subject to the same laws of physical nature as we are. He experienced hunger, thirst, and the need to rest.

He also was subject to many of the same laws of human nature as we are. Perhaps that's why He had to be alone from time to time. As a human, He must also have tired of having the disciples around day and night for three years. He not only heard their arguing and bickering about who was going to sit where in heaven (Mark 10:35-41), but He also knew their thoughts (Luke 9:46-48). Knowing what was in their hearts must have caused Him some pain.

Often Jesus encouraged adults to learn from children.

Nevertheless, there was one group of people I'm certain Jesus would have welcomed any time: the children. Often He encouraged adults to learn from children, saying we need to be like them to enter the kingdom of God. (Matt. 18:1-6.) And on one very special occasion, He allowed us to know the depths of His concern for the little ones:

Some people brought their small children to Jesus so he could touch them. But his followers told the people to stop bringing their children to him. When Jesus saw this, he was displeased. He said to them, "Let the little children come to me. Don't stop them. The kingdom of God belongs to people who are like these little children. I tell you the truth. You must accept the kingdom of God as a little child accepts things, or you will never enter it." Then Jesus took the children in his arms. He put his hands on them and blessed them.

MARK 10:13-16

Taking these children in His arms, placing His hands on them, and blessing them was not at all an unfamiliar behavior to Jesus or to those around Him. He was simply doing what a good Jewish father or rabbi would have done. His action was a lesson to His listeners then and to us today about the significance of children and the need to actively communicate God as Father to them.

Blessing children is as vital today as it was in Jesus' time.

At times I've thought, *Oh, to have been one of those children that Jesus held in His arms and blessed.* But, in all likelihood, those little children were not aware of the significance of that experience. Though Jesus is the Son of God and His blessing was certainly precious, the greatest value of His one-time blessing of the children may well have been that it taught the adults who watched how they should treat their children. For those who followed His example, the most important blessings their children would receive were those they received from their families thereafter.

Blessing our children is as vital in today's world as it was in Jesus' time. With temptations in our society pulling at them from all directions, children need a wall of protection surrounding them. And the earlier we begin strengthening that wall, the safer they'll be when the temptations come.

The wall they need is provided by our love. It can be reinforced, brick by brick, each time we bless them.

MAY THE LORD ANSWER YOU WHEN

you are in distress; may the name

of the God of Jacob protect you.

May he send you help and grant you support.

May he give you the desire of your heart

and make all your plans succeed.

May the Lord grant all your requests.

ADAPTED FROM PSALM 20:1,2,4,5 NIV

CHAPTER FOUR

MAKING IT WORK

It's been determined that the blessing is an ancient biblical practice that countless parents through the ages have maintained as valuable and even indispensable. Nevertheless, at this point I can anticipate the question: But does it *work*?

If "work" means some mechanical connection between the blessing and certain immediate, specific behaviors of children, that would be difficult to prove. Any connection of that nature would amount to little more than manipulation.

However, a useful measure of the positive impact of practicing the blessing can be found in children's attitudes toward the blessings in homes where it is practiced. In our home, an occasional situation has provided a telling anecdote that illustrated just how much Carlton and Lisa valued the blessing.

THE SECURITY OF THE BLESSING

During one particular time in my life, when work required international travel lasting from two to five weeks, I called home to bless the children about once a week. On the eve of one of those trips, I was tucking eleven-year-old Lisa into bed when she asked, "Dad, how long will you be gone on this trip?"

"Oh," I said, "about four or five weeks."

"No," she persisted. "How many nights will you be gone—exactly?" I went to count on my calendar the exact number of nights, then returned to her room.

"Thirty-two nights," I said. "Why?"

"Well," Lisa mused, "then you have to give me thirty-two blessings. Now."

I chuckled as I considered her request, but I thought, *Why not?* So I agreed. Anticipating that this would take a while, I lay down beside her as I placed my hand on her head. Then I began: "The Lord bless you and keep you, Lisa. . . . " I went on to say the full blessing from Numbers 6:24-26 that I had spoken over her for years.

When I was done, Lisa said, "That's one, Dad. You've got thirty-one more to go!"

Some time later, when I finished the last one (with Lisa counting all the way), she chirped, "Okay, Dad. Now you can go on your trip." The job was done. Lisa felt secure. She knew everything would be fine, even though Dad was a long way from home. Of course, the fact that I spoke the blessing to her thirty-two times was no more powerful than speaking it once to her in faith.

However, my blessing for every night represented to her the security of my commitment to her welfare.

As you consider how children's positive attitudes toward the family blessing indicate its significance in their lives, you might wonder whether the particular words spoken really mean anything to the children themselves, especially if they're young. You might conclude that all the kids are actually responding to is the fact that they're receiving a few undivided moments of parental attention.

I agree that one critical factor in the blessing's ability to convey God's love to kids is the parental attention, which they desperately need. However, many children also listen carefully to what's being said.

One friend of mine has been blessing his children every night for several years now. He began one night with a simple "God bless you with grace and peace in Jesus' name. Amen." But over the following few months, as he considered all the kinds of blessing he wanted his children to experience, the list grew. Now each night he lays his hands on his children and imparts:

God bless you with grace and peace,
power and protection,
health and healing,
holiness and godliness,
abundance and prosperity,

and all the fruit and gifts of the Holy Spirit,
in Jesus' name. Amen.

That's a formidable list of blessings to remember, even for an adult, and it's only because they are repeated each night that he's able to call them to mind.

Nevertheless, one evening my friend was exhausted from a particularly demanding day, and as he blessed his children, he accidentally forgot a portion of the blessings. Immediately his young daughter interrupted.

"Dad," she insisted, "don't forget the power and protection. That's important."

Even a six-year-old was paying close attention, knowing that every word was important.

In our high-tech world, we're becoming more and more conditioned to expect the instantaneous. But I'm a little skeptical of techniques that promise instant changes in our children. No doubt the results of blessing our children, or anyone else, are *sometimes* visible immediately. But usually results of these blessings come much later. And sometimes only God is the witness.

THE CHINESE BAMBOO TREE

Zig Ziglar tells the story of the Chinese bamboo tree. When the seed is planted, instead of sending up a shoot, it goes dormant. No amount of nurture and attention can rouse it from its sleep.

The Chinese bamboo lies dormant for five years with no apparent signs of growth. Then in one year it suddenly grows over sixty feet into a mature tree.

Even though the tree reveals no visible signs of growth for several years, it still requires the care that would be given to any other seed. Without such care during its incubation, it would never become a tree. Since the farmers know this, they continue to care for the seed—despite the lack of any visible results.[1] Kids can be like Chinese bamboo trees. As parents we may do everything we know is right, but then we may despair if we don't witness any immediate growth or change of heart. Sometimes we even become so anxious over their progress that we "dig them up" with our frustration and undo the good we've done.

This situation may be especially frustrating when a child has once made a commitment to the Lord. Often when the teenage years arrive, those sweet, obedient children may begin to question and rebel against both their parents and their faith. They may even appear to be going full speed in the wrong direction, doing things they know are wrong.

How should a parent respond if that happens? Should you force them to accept your faith "or else . . . "? Or do you keep on "hoeing" around them, tending to the things you know will produce a mature tree someday?

God desires to lavish Himself on us and reward our obedience to Him.

Though it's easy to give up at such a time, we must keep in mind that we really want our kids to have their *own* faith in God, not their *parents'* faith. Sometimes the transfer of faith is swift and smooth; sometimes it's slow and painful. But if we stay the course, prayerfully doing what we know is right, sooner or later the tree will grow, and when it does, it will be strong and well rooted.

Your commitment to continue blessing your children during these difficult months or years shows them an element of your faith they might never see otherwise. Your steady, unwavering demonstration of confidence in what they'll become will help them mature in accordance with those positive expectations.

THE BENEFITS OF THE BLESSING

I want to affirm that God desires to lavish Himself on us and reward our obedience to Him openly and abundantly—and, at times, quickly. His reward comes to us in many ways, as His promises indicate:

He will meet all our needs. (Phil. 4:19.)

He will give us the desires of our hearts. (Ps. 37:4.)

He will send angels to guard us. (Ps. 91:11.)

He will withhold no good thing. (Ps. 84:11.)

One of the benefits of blessing our children is an element of openness and honesty, both toward us and toward God.

This has been illustrated through the years by the candor they've shown in confessing things they've done that they knew were wrong.

I remember one particular night, when Carlton was about eleven years old, he called us to his room. We had tucked him in for the night, prayed with him, and given him his "hands-on" blessing. But, alone in the dark, he had been thinking about something he had done that day. He knew that what he had done was wrong, and God would not, as the blessing said, "give him peace" until he confessed and made things right.

It didn't take long for the confession to come and the tears to flow. We listened as he prayed and asked God to forgive him and help him not to do that again. We talked with him and assured him that God had heard his prayer and forgiven him. We verbally forgave him also. Then we prayed again with him.

As we were walking to the door, he said, "Mom and Dad, I feel like a big bag of junk just left me!" Mary and I rejoiced with him in his release from guilt, and we knew that God was at work in him. We have marveled again and again at how both of our children have remained open with us about what's going on in their lives.

Our greatest responsibility to our children is to exhibit the heart of God to them.

Earlier we noted that our greatest responsibility to God as Christian parents is to raise children to know and love Him with all their hearts. At the same time, our greatest responsibility to our children is to exhibit the heart of God to them. What they see in us has great bearing on what they understand God to be like.

When we have something we dearly treasure, we take special care of it, making certain that it's not damaged or destroyed. We accord it a place of honor and would never consider taking out our frustration or anger on such a treasure. Instead, we protect it in every way possible.

The same is true of our children. After years of reinforcing their sense of security, acceptance, and self-esteem through blessing, the last thing we want to do is destroy what we've worked so diligently to cultivate. So the blessing of our children becomes a daily reminder that we have built a relationship with them and an attitude within them that must be protected—even when we have reason to be angry.

When my son was young, I bought a new car that was by far the nicest car I had ever owned, and certainly the most expensive. I loved that car and took special care of it, washing it frequently and maintaining it faithfully.

When we have something we dearly treasure, we take special care of it.

One spring morning, however, I noticed a footprint on the hood. Upon closer inspection, I also saw a dent in the hood where the footprint was.

There was little question that it was Carlton's footprint. My heart sank and my anger rose. I'm now grateful that he had already left for school! As I stood by the front of the car, I wondered why he would have climbed on the hood. Then I spotted my golf clubs on the shelf above the front of the car, remembered the warm spring weather, and understood what had happened.

As I drove to work, I noticed that the dent in the hood was right in my line of vision so that every time I sat behind the wheel of that car, I would see it. Because it was in such a prominent place, my immediate thought was to get it fixed. After all, isn't that what insurance is for?

Nevertheless, in my heart I heard the Lord saying, *Just leave it. It's not that bad, and besides, the car's not yours anyway. It's mine. Everything you have is mine. And so is your family.*

I thought of the close relationship I'd built with my son, and how much I treasured him. Then I thought of how close I'd come to allowing something else I treasured—something of infinitely less value—to hurt that relationship. I had blessed my son for years; was I going to "curse" him with hurtful words now?

No. Instead, I felt God telling me, *Why not use that dent as a positive reminder that your son needs your prayer?* After all, the Lord had given me this boy so I could care for him, pray for him, and show him the heart of his heavenly Father.

Years later that old car expired. It had clocked 128,000 miles by the time it died, and nearly as many prayers of gratitude for God's goodness in giving me my son.

I did question Carlton about the dent. He had no idea of what he'd done. He'd simply acted impulsively on his desire to swing the golf clubs. So he apologized, asked me to forgive him, and agreed to use the stepladder next time. Needless to say, our relationship was stronger than ever before.

Does the blessing of your children work? Is it worth the time and commitment? The answer is clear: Yes! Absolutely!

Is the blessing of your children worth the time and commitment?

Our experience and that of many other families show that the blessing works. Of course, just *how* it works is more difficult to explain. We can observe the sense of security and concern that is obviously produced by speaking words of encouragement to a child, day after day, and recognize that such encouragement is bound to impact the child's life for good. But blessing him or her seems to convey much more.

As the ancient Hebrews recognized, words of blessing spoken in the name of God are able to transmit the power and favor of God.

Those who have faithfully spoken it year after year would probably all agree on one point: Blessing others is practiced *because it is the right thing to do.* Based on the examples given in

Scripture, God rewards those who bless as well as those who are being blessed.

God rewards those who bless as well as those who are being blessed.

Up to this point, this book has illustrated the significant difference a regular blessing can make in the lives of children. But perhaps children can provide the most convincing testimonies of what the blessing can mean to them. Following are recent letters written to me by my children, Carlton and Lisa. Their words reflect the importance of receiving the blessing now that they are both grown with children of their own.

Dear Dad,

The past few days I've been thinking a lot about the blessing and what it means to me now as a 32-year-old father. As I've reflected, I think of the blessing in a new way.

First, I think of it in its pure simplicity as I bless my ten-year-old daughter, Christina, and its impact on her. I can remember receiving a blessing from you every day as I grew up. I can remember being a scared little kid who needed comfort and reassuring, but the blessing brought peace to my heart. This is something I wanted to do for my own child. I knew how much it meant to me to know that my parents loved me enough to ask God to bless me every day, and I really feel like He did.

I have been blessing Christina every day since she was born. It has become a ritual in our house, as it was for me when I was a kid. She asks for it like I did and reminds me if I forget—like I did to you. Our own little blessing dynamic has evolved ever since she started attending school. We went to two-a-day—a very demanding schedule! I started blessing her every morning in the car on the way to school after we pray for the day. This always seems to start her day well.

Sometimes I was a little jealous. Maybe I don't have a tough spelling test or a class bully to deal with, but you know, I could still use a blessing too! So shortly after that, she began blessing me as well—each morning and each night before bed. There are many days that I think it means more to hear those words from her than it is for her to hear them from me.

I asked her recently what she thought about getting blessings every day. I had never asked her that before. I asked her to just quickly write down what came to her. She thought about it for a minute, and this is what she wrote: "It makes me feel so good. It helps me sleep and feel safe. It makes me happy and have happy thoughts, not nightmares—I sleep like a log. When I get a blessing in the morning, it gives me courage and makes me feel strong when I start the day. It brightens my day. I feel good when I bless my dad because I feel like it helps him through the day and it helps to take away pain." She couldn't be more right.

The other aspect of the blessing that I've realized in the past few years is the impact of our words on our kids and on others. I feel that hearing those warm, loving words every day builds a strong self-image and high self-esteem.

So many people are beat up with words from angry, hurtful people, and many times, those people are their own parents. How much better it is to fill our kids' hearts and ears with words of love! The blessing provides a special time with my little girl twice a day to express that to her.

Dad, I remember that day in Chicago when I heard you speak about the blessing at a church there. It was the only time I've heard you talk to a group of people about this personal thing you did with your family. I was really moved that day when I saw how many people want to have kind words—blessed words from God spoken to them by the people they love most. I was also saddened by how many had never heard those words before that day. I think it can be life changing for families to start doing this for each other every day, whether they're 10 or 110.

Thank you, Dad, for giving me loving words and actions to back them up.

—Carlton

Dear Dad,

The blessing was such a special gift that you gave us; it was free, yet so valuable! I never tired of receiving the blessing or the big hug that went along with it. I felt so affirmed, secure, accepted, and loved.

It took only a minute—but what a powerful sixty seconds! It was a bonding time and a time of reconciliation that brought a peaceful closure to each day. That consistency brought such security. You never withheld your blessing as punishment. Your willingness to give us your blessing was not dependent upon our behavior, because the blessing was not a reward to be earned. It was a gift. Knowing that we would be receiving a blessing before we went to bed gave us an opportunity that we could count on to talk about what was on our hearts, to bring resolution to any conflicts earlier in the day, or just to say "I love you."

The blessing is not a mere physical thing, a duty, or meaningless words; it is imparting God's favor. So often as you spoke the blessing I sensed the Lord's presence. He would bring life and authority to your words as you spoke them. I am convinced that it is because of the blessing that it was so easy for me to know Jesus personally. It helped me know His love for me as an individual. It also taught me to receive God's gifts and not strive to earn them, as my role in the blessing was all about receiving. Lastly, I believe it helped to shape my image of God. I always pictured Jesus with a smile on His face and His arms outstretched beckoning me to come to Him. I know this stems from the warmth, love, and joy over me which you expressed as you blessed me. This made it easy to view my heavenly Father in the same way.

Dad, you did your part in faithfully pronouncing the blessing, but God also did His part in accomplishing every aspect of the blessing in my life. He truly has blessed me and kept me faithful to Him, shown me His face and His grace, and given me His peace. Thank you, Dad, for leaving this legacy for us to follow.

I now have the joy of continuing this legacy with my own kids. It has been such a joy to speak the blessing over Sofie and Elle. Sofie already, at the age of two, says the whole blessing perfectly and often blesses mom and dad in return. I am so grateful that my husband has also embraced the vision of blessing our children daily. We look forward to seeing the fruit of it in their lives, as I have certainly seen in my own life.

—Lisa

THEN SOME CHILDREN WERE

brought to Him so that He might lay

His hands on them and pray. . . .

MATTHEW 19:13

CHAPTER FIVE

GETTING STARTED

And be gracious to you.

The most difficult part of any job for me is getting started.

Sometimes the tasks I delay are as simple as replacing a light bulb. I can rationalize, excuse, and defend this behavior with comments like, "We can see just fine without that light," or "Do you realize how much it costs to burn that thing?" or best of all, "What good will it do? It's just going to burn out again anyway!"

Finally, when I complete the job, I find not only that the bulb took all of two minutes to replace, but also that it really is nice to have the extra light. Getting started with the blessing of your children is a little like replacing a light bulb. It really isn't much work when you actually do it; it doesn't take much time, and the results are better than you thought. But I can't give you a simple formula that says, "Do these five things, and all your troubles will end." You see, there's no right or wrong way to bless your children. A blessing of any sort is still a blessing—something good and powerful and precious. The only mistake you can make is to decide that for fear of doing something wrong you'll do nothing at all.

There's no right or wrong way to bless your children.

Let's explore some of the common questions in getting started.

1. *What age should my children be when I start and stop the family blessing?*

The answer is simple. At what age do you want them to begin receiving the benefits of being blessed, and how long do you want that to continue?

It's not important whether they're fifteen years or fifteen months, or whether or not they understand the words you are speaking. The longer you wait to begin, the fewer opportunities you will have to impart God's grace to them through the family blessing.

Take full advantage of the time you have—start today. The overwhelming majority of all we will ever learn in life, we learn before we start school. Of course, all is not lost if that time in our children's lives is past. God can and will impart His blessings. But nothing can be gained by further delay.

By the same token, children are never too old to be blessed. They need the favor and power of God throughout their lives. So why would we ever stop the family blessing?

Older kids I know who have been blessed since an early age don't consider it a childish ritual they've outgrown. On the contrary, they now cherish the blessing more than ever. So even if children move far away, they can be blessed daily, long distance in our private prayer times.

2. *Is bedtime the only time of day to bless my children?*

Absolutely not. God is up and awake all the time and is always ready to bless. Since it's God who actually does the blessing, any time is the right time.

However, structure and consistency are important, especially to young children. So think through your day and find the best time for your family. It may be bedtime or mealtime. It may even be when your children leave for school so they can launch out on the new day with a blessing still ringing in their ears.

If the best time for your family isn't immediately obvious, experiment a bit. Tell your kids what you want to do and why. If they're older, ask for their suggestions.

3. *Should the blessing be spoken daily?*

Take full advantage of the time you have—start today.

Again, there are no rules; however, a daily blessing obviously gives you more opportunities to bless your kids.

Many families prefer to have a regular time of family blessing on a weekly basis.

4. *How do I know what to say?*

Take a look at the blessings that end each chapter. One of these might meet your needs. Or try using a concordance to find all the occurrences of the word *bless* in the Bible; among them you'll find a number of blessings, and you'll learn a great deal as well about how blessings were given in biblical times. Of course, there is always the option of creating your own blessing based on Scripture. When we agree with God's Word, we know we are in agreement with His will.

5. *Does the blessing have to be the same every time?*

Not at all. You can vary the blessing however you see fit.

As I mentioned earlier, structure and consistency are important, especially for younger children. There is a certain value to repeating the same words over and over again every night of a child's growing-up years; it provides them a sense of stability, of predictableness, of security. You don't need to seek novelty for its own sake. But if you think a fresh form of the blessing would benefit your children, why not try a different one? You may even want to learn a whole series of blessings based on Scripture and rotate them regularly. In fact, the blessing doesn't have to have a set form at all. Like prayer, it can be spontaneous.

6. *Who should provide the blessing in the family?*

There is no one answer. As Christians we're all called to bless and be a blessing. In our family, as the husband and father, I assumed the primary responsibility of blessing our children, but Mary often joined me. She also spoke the blessing to the kids in my absence. Some families prefer to have both parents give the blessing together. In single-parent homes, it should be the spiritual head of the household, whether that is a mother or a father. Even our children have given the blessing to each other.

7. *Does blessing your children replace prayer?*

Definitely not. There are three vital kinds of conversation with God that we share with our children. These conversations are like strands woven together to form a single braid which collectively are infinitely stronger than individually. On this braid, I believe, hang all the other disciplines we desire to develop in our children's Christian lives. And though the three are similar, they serve very distinct purposes.

Strand One:

Prayer *for* our children—interceding for them as the family's priest, lifting them and their needs up to the throne of God.

Strand Two:

Prayer *with* our children—introducing them to God, bringing them into our own conversations with God, modeling for them a healthy pattern of regular communication with the Father.

Strand Three:

Blessing our children—to complement and strengthen the other two, reflecting the goodness, power, and the fatherly heart of the God we talk to when we pray for and with our children.

When you begin the practice of blessing your children, here are a few guidelines:

1. *Before you begin, explain to children old enough to understand what you're planning to do and why you believe it's important.*

Children will be much more cooperative and appreciative if they understand why you want to bless them and why it's important. Provide answers to their questions as well as you can.

A dear friend of mine was visiting with me one evening. As we began talking about our kids, I told him about our practice and of the benefits of blessing our children. He liked the idea and decided to begin blessing his three children, who were ten, eight, and four at the time.

Nearly a year later I saw him again, and he could hardly wait to tell me the news. "Guess what? I've been blessing my children ever since we were together last time. It's great! I went home, took each one in my arms individually, put my hand on the child's head, and gave the blessing from Numbers 6."

He was grinning widely as he told his story. "You know," he observed, "each of the children responds differently when I bless them. One gets right into it. He snuggles up to me when I hold him and almost purrs in the process. The second one just receives it nonchalantly, as a normal part of what Dad does. But the little guy stands at attention. His arms are at his sides, and he's stiff as a soldier. To him, this is God touching him, and he wants to be as good as he can."

The kids each had a different understanding of what the blessing was about. But the important point is that from the beginning, each one had some understanding of what was going on that held meaning for him or her.

2. *Hold your children in your arms when you bless them.*

Gary Smalley and John Trent have an excellent chapter in their book, *The Blessing,* called "The First Element of the Blessing: Meaningful Touch." In it they chronicle the value of parents touching their children, citing examples and teaching from a spiritual, psychological, and physical perspective.

Hugging has always been as much a part of my extended family as saying "hello" or "good-bye." We virtually never do one without the other. Whichever family member is involved makes no difference. Whenever we greet or leave one another, we hug.

In fact, I hug almost anybody. When I hug folks who aren't family members, I often hear them comment, "Oh, I really needed that!"

One of my son's buddies, a hard-working, no-nonsense, super-jock type, came to our house some time ago, and I gave him a hug. When I let him go, he said, "I like coming to the Garborgs' house. They give hugs here." Now he also gives me hugs on Sundays after church.

From reading the Bible, we can conclude that the patriarchs knew the value of touching. Jesus knew the value of it as well. He took the little children in His arms and held them when He blessed them. We should too. It's a way of telling children that we accept them as they are, and it opens the door for them to receive the blessing when we give it to them.

From reading the Bible, we can conclude that the patriarchs knew the value of touching.

At the same time it's important to note that some people feel uncomfortable hugging others. Perhaps their families were not especially affectionate physically or certain experiences in their lives have caused them to resist close contact of the sort I am describing here. That's okay. A hand on the shoulder or on the arm can be a meaningful substitute. I would, however, encourage you to explore ways in which you can experience the closeness that can only come through a more physical expression of affection.

3. *Place your hand or hands on the heads of your children when you bless them.*

This action is also modeled to us by Jesus. And no wonder—the gesture has great spiritual significance and symbolism connected with it.

The Bible teaches that the "laying on of hands" was used for consecrating people for service to God, imparting the Holy Spirit, and praying for the sick to be healed. In the church today, it's also used in the symbolic gestures of baptism, confirmation, and ordination.

Larry Lenning, in his book *Blessing in Mosque and Mission,* notes that in the biblical context:

> the act of laying on of hands was a sacred act through which the blessings of God were given. The hands of the blesser were not sacred. But through these human instruments, God bestowed His benediction, power, grace and mercy. . . . In the light of the Jewish background of the New Testament and the early Church and with the evidence of the New Testament itself, the laying on of hands was a sacred act through which God bestowed varied blessings.[1]

The symbolism of "covering" our children is important here. We depict to them through this gesture the protection and care with which God shields them.

4. *Always include in your blessing an invocation of the name of God.*

It's the name of the one true God that separates this blessing from all other blessings in the religions of the world. Many non-Christian cultures have forms of blessing similar in intent and wording to those of the Christian faith. What sets the Christian blessing apart as a divinely powerful experience is the invoking of the name of the true God. When we contemplate the sheer awesomeness of God and the infiniteness of His power, we can begin to understand what can happen at the mere mention of His name. And we can identify with David's feelings when he cried out to God in Psalm 103:1 NAS: "Bless the Lord, O my soul; and all that is within me, bless His holy *name*."

The form of God's name you use is, of course, up to you, according to what is most meaningful to your family. Many Christians use the church's tradition of invoking God with the name of the Holy Trinity: "In the name of the Father, and of the Son, and of the Holy Spirit." Others prefer simply "in Jesus' name." In either case, the powerful name of our Lord sets apart our blessing as a vessel of *His* grace.

5. *Teach your children to speak blessings on themselves on days when you forget or are unable to give the blessing for some reason. Help them understand that the blessing of God still rests on them and protects them.*

Younger children especially look forward to the comfort and security of the blessing, and they may become unsettled if it's not given for whatever reason. It is important to avoid encouraging kids to think that God's blessing, and especially His protection, comes only through the spoken words of a parent. If we emphasize to young ones that the family blessing is simply one of many ways the Lord pours out His favor and power and that they have the privilege of speaking blessing as well, then we can allow them to feel secure in God's love and in our own.

Here's a brief review of the main points we've made in this chapter to help you get started:

- Start today, no matter the age of your children.
- Bedtime is a good time to bless your kids, but by no means the only time. Explore what works best for your family, with regard to the time of day and frequency of the blessing.
- Choose words for your blessing by referring to the suggestions in this book or finding them in Scripture. The words don't necessarily have to be the same every time, though there are benefits to continuity.
- Blessing should never take the place of prayer. Blessing, prayer *for* your children, and prayer *with* your children are all important ways of including children in our conversations with God.
- Explain to your children what you're doing and why.

- Hold your children in your arms when you bless them, and place your hand or hands on their heads.
- Always invoke the name of God in your blessing.
- Teach your children that the family blessing is only one of the ways God uses to bless and protect us.
- Above all, begin today!

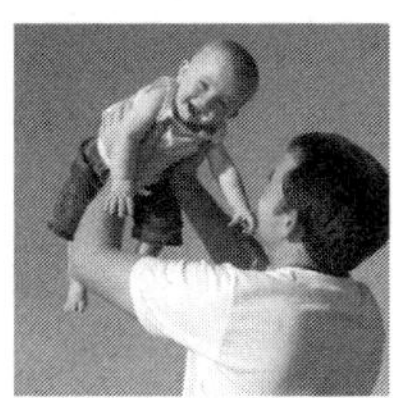

THE GOD OF LOVE AND PEACE

will be with you. May the grace of the

Lord Jesus Christ, and the love of God,

and the fellowship of the

Holy Spirit be with you all.

2 CORINTHIANS 13:11,14 NIV

CHAPTER SIX

A POSITIVE COVERING

So far we've focused on blessing in a specific sense: the kind of blessing we read about in the Bible in which one person intentionally and explicitly invokes the goodness of God into the life of another person through the spoken word. Now we'll explore the blessing in a more general sense: how the power of words operates in our daily lives to strengthen or to hurt those around us—not just within family relationships, but within all relationships.

We know God is a God of blessing; the Bible makes that clear. But the Bible also shows that God's people are to be a *people of blessing.* In Matthew 5:44, Jesus commanded us not only to bless our loved ones, but to bless our enemies as well. The Lord pours out His power and favor on us, and like Abraham, He appoints us to be a blessing. He has delegated to us the role of conveying His grace to others, and one of the primary means by which we can do this is through the power of our daily words.

Jesus commanded us to bless our loved ones as well as our enemies.

"Death and life," says the book of Proverbs, "are in the power of the tongue" (18:21 NAS). Nowhere is this reality clearer than in the dynamics of family life. The words parents speak to their children day in and day out, even in casual conversation, create an atmosphere in the home over time that either choke and poison their young spirits or nourish and strengthen them. The results can be devastating or life giving: "Reckless words pierce like a sword, but the tongue of the wise brings healing" (Prov. 12:18 NIV).

We have the daily choice as parents to speak life or death to our children. Speaking "death"—destroying their self-esteem with negative labels, nicknames, household reputations, or self-fulfilling prophecies—is what the Bible calls "cursing"; we will deal with that issue specifically in chapter seven. But even if we rarely inflict these kinds of verbal injuries on our children, we may still be guilty of draining the life from their spirits by our negligence or reluctance to "speak well" of them.

We have the daily choice as parents to speak life or death to our children.

SPEAKING EULOGIES

Just think about the English word for "speaking well" of someone that comes from the Greek root *eulogeo: eulogy.* When do people present eulogies? At the person's funeral! It's sad that we wait until people are gone before we eulogize them, before we "speak of them well."

Proverbs 25:11 NKJV says, "A word fitly spoken is like apples of gold in settings of silver." An appropriate expression of appreciation is an adornment placed on the recipient that brings honor to the person, whether alone or in the presence of others. Now is the best time to adorn our children with such blessings.

This general kind of blessing is not limited to words spoken *about* our children. It can also refer to the words we use when speaking to them. Words that show respect can elevate their self-esteem, their level of performance, and their attitude.

I've heard business managers give commands to their associates as though they were some sort of drill sergeant, rather than use a polite request. Whenever workers are told, "Do this" or "Bring me that," their morale and productivity suffer. If we would consider what a difference could be made by prefacing our requests with a genuine, "Would you mind" or "Could you please," we could create a more joyful, efficient workplace. Then, when the job is finished, a "Thank you" or "I appreciate what you did" could be an added blessing.

If kind words are appropriate in the workplace, they're even more appropriate at home.

If kind words are appropriate in the workplace, they're even more appropriate at home. Family blessings often take on the form of a kind word prefacing a request. Look at what Paul essentially says in

Ephesians 4:29: "When you talk, do not say harmful things. But say what people need—words that will help others become stronger. Then what you say will help those who listen to you." These kind words can be said in private or public. They will always be appreciated and could often result in changed behavior on the part of the recipient. First Peter 3:8-9 illustrates the very nature of blessing:

> *Finally, all of you should live together in peace. Try to understand each other. Love each other as brothers. Be kind and humble. Do not do wrong to a person to pay him back for doing wrong to you. Or do not insult someone to pay him back for insulting you. But ask God to bless that person. Do this, because you yourselves were called to receive a blessing.*

Of course, the reason we bless our children or anyone else by speaking well of them is not to control them or to squeeze a little more from them. We bless people because it's the right thing to do! Period. Receiving a blessing in return is simply a bonus that God provides for obeying Him.

WORDS THAT ARE WARRANTED AND SINCERE

In order for a blessing of this type (the kind word or expression of praise) to be well received, it must meet at least two conditions. First, it must be *warranted.* You may have to think hard to find a quality you can praise in someone—even, at times, your own child. Keep looking; you'll find it. An unwarranted blessing is empty and hollow. It's not really a blessing at all.

For a blessing to be well received, it must be warranted and sincere.

The second condition for a genuine blessing of this sort is that it must be *sincere.* An insincere compliment is easily detected, and it leaves a bitter taste in the mouth of both the giver and the receiver. But a sincere compliment does more to build the confidence of those around us than almost anything else we can do.

During the early spring of our son's senior year in high school, Mary and I were talking with the parents of some of his classmates. His school was a small Christian institution with a graduating class of only eleven. Several of these kids had actually been together since they'd started school a dozen years earlier.

We were reflecting on how the parents of those kids had bonded as well. We had all watched them grow. Four of the boys had played sports together since the seventh grade. We had witnessed the character development that comes from teamwork and competition, as well as seen their development as friends and as Christians.

As we reminisced about the uniqueness of this class of eleven, a desire to do something special developed. We decided to have an "Appreciation Night." We did not realize at the time how powerful the evening would become and the impact it would have on everyone present.

Only the parents and their senior-class children were present. Many schedule adjustments had to be made: business meetings, sports practices, and homework. The conversation over dinner was light and relaxed. Following the meal, the program began. There were plenty of laughs as we "roasted" each senior. Then the room drew quiet.

One by one, each father came to the front and declared to his child those things that he most appreciated about him or her. Many tears were exchanged between father and son or father and daughter. One dad prefaced his words with a confession: "I have never really told you this before. . . . "

Each father's list of comments was specific and individual, making them much more meaningful. Their "words fitly spoken" included treasures such as these:

"You are the type of daughter, the type of person, who has helped me grow."

"You have a heart for God."

"God will reward you for all the hidden sacrifices you have made."

"My only regret is that I didn't have ten more just like you!"

"I see the treasures God has put in you beginning to blossom."

"I see Jesus in you."

These fathers' heartfelt remarks were "eulogies" in the best sense of the word—expressions of praise given before it was too late. Their power to bless their children was intensified because these words were spoken by someone significant in their lives: their fathers.

At the end of each comment, father and child embraced. In conclusion, the blessing found in Numbers 6:24-26 was sung to the tune a father had written.

That evening provided the opportunity for feelings of gratitude and encouragement to flow—in some cases, perhaps, feelings that hadn't been expressed in years.

If you haven't been regularly blessing your children with kind words that come from a heart of gratitude, start now. Begin speaking well of them and expressing praise to them today. Desire the best for your children by taking the initiative. Make an active commitment to bless your family daily, allowing God to do His part.

THE LORD WATCHES OVER YOU—

the Lord is your shade at your right hand;

the sun will not harm you by day,

nor the moon by night.

The Lord will keep you from all harm—

he will watch over your life;

the Lord will watch over your coming

and going both now and forevermore.

PSALM 121:5-8 NIV

CHAPTER SEVEN

YOU CAN'T SAW SAWDUST

The Lord lift up his countenance on you.

"Let bygones be bygones." "No use crying over spilled milk." "What's done is done." "You can't turn back the clock."

These are just a few of the clichés we tell ourselves for comfort when we think of all the things we wish we had done differently in life, or not done at all. And they all contain sound advice. Even the apostle Paul dealt this way with his past: "But one thing I do," he wrote, "forgetting what is behind . . . " (Phil. 3:13 NIV). He didn't sit around mourning what he had done in the days before his conversion.

Nevertheless, Paul did more about his past than just put it behind him. He also used it as an inspiration for the future. He learned from his experiences, both good and bad, success and failure. So he went on to affirm: "I press on. . . . "

In light of Paul's words, take another look at the sayings just quoted. Though each attempts to encourage, none really succeed; they all stop short of what Paul said. Unlike Paul's statement, they fail to offer any hope for the future. Bygones really *are* bygones. What's done is done. And maybe you don't have to cry over spilled milk—but whether you cry or not, you still have to wipe it up.

Perhaps you've felt a bit guilty or remorseful as you've read this book because you didn't bless your kids when they were young, and now they're not living at home anymore. Maybe you feel as if you "blew" it, not just in blessing your kids, but in your parenting role in general. Or you might even be feeling a bit wistful about your own childhood and your relationship to your parents, because you know that as a child you didn't receive the blessing yourself.

If any of these things are true in your case, you may have been telling yourself, "Oh, well, no use cryin' over spilled milk. It's too late. There's nothing I can do now."

That's not at all true. Actually, there's a great deal more you can do, even now. That's why I like another expression better than all the ones we mentioned. Some folks say, "You can't saw sawdust." Maybe not, but there's plenty you can make out of it.

MAKING PARTICLEBOARD OF THE PAST

For years lumber mills had few uses for the sawdust they were creating when they cut up their logs. Most of it just went to waste.

Then researchers discovered that by mixing the sawdust with resin and compressing it, they could make a product that was stronger and less expensive than the original. Particleboard was born. As a result, sawdust is now being used extensively in all types of construction today.

A similar invention rescues waste scraps of leather. Did you know that there are no fewer than fifty different materials used in Bible covers? We cover the Word with pigskin, sheepskin, cowhide, and calfhide; durabond, leatherflex, skivertex, and kivar; chevo, croupon, rexine, and roncote, to name just a few. But by far the most popular deluxe binding for Bibles is called "bonded leather."

This material is made up of all the leftover scraps of genuine leather used in other Bible covers; the scraps are reprocessed and mixed with special resins. The result is a versatile new material that has all the qualities of the original leather but at a lower cost.

When you think of your past as a child or as a parent, think about that particleboard or the bonded leather. Have you considered how you might be able to make something new out of what's left over?

Perhaps you feel that the opportunity to be blessed by your parents or to bless your own children has passed, and that there's nothing you can do to go back in time and change it all. As a youngster you may have been a model child, or a rebel who turned your folks' hair gray. As a parent you may have used the time when your kids were young to shape their character and values, or you may have blown it completely. You may have just sailed through your childhood or your parenthood, blissfully unaware of all that could have been different, happy as a clam at high tide just to have survived.

The past cannot be changed, but you can change the ongoing effects of what happened.

In one sense, it really doesn't matter now. It's done. You're grown and out of your parents' home. Or your kids are grown and out of your home. The past cannot be changed, but you can change the ongoing effects of what happened. You can't saw sawdust, but you can make something of great value and usefulness out of it.

A SAWDUST MASTERPIECE

Years ago, I was admiring a beautiful sculpture that belonged to my sister-in-law and her husband. The artwork was the bust of a bald eagle entitled "In God We Trust."

The artist is Mario Fernandez, a Cuban refugee who entered the U.S. with nothing more than the clothes on his back and the American dream. In his native land, Mario had spent two years in prison as a young political dissenter. For him, the American dream represented everything that couldn't possibly be realized in Cuba. He had only been able to fulfill that dream through his strong faith in God. That's the reason behind the sculpture "In God We Trust."

Soon after admiring Mario's eagle, Mary and I received one as a gift from her sister and her husband. When I discovered what this gorgeous, hand-painted, limited edition bust of the bald eagle was created from, I was shocked. It was made from sawdust—sawdust mixed with resin, given value by the skill of an artist.

As I reflected on the nature of particleboard, bonded leather, and Mario's masterpiece, I saw the parallels between them and the possibilities of our own lives. In all of these cases, three things are necessary to create something new from scraps of the old:

1. An awareness of the value of the old, leftover scraps, no matter what their condition.
2. A resin to hold the material together.
3. A vision in the creator of what those scraps can become, whether the new creation is particleboard, bonded leather, a work of art, or a new relationship with our parents or children.

No matter what your past relationship with your parents or children has been, you can start with a clean slate today. Even if there was abuse, neglect, hypocrisy, or any number of destructive forms of behavior, those things are sawdust now, and it's up to you what you'll do with that sawdust. You can sweep it up and throw it out, saying, "Good riddance!" or you can say, "Look at this mess! What can I make out of this?"

God is the Master Artist who can look at those old, leftover scraps and see the finished product as a work of art, a new creation of precious value. And God desires to take these "scraps" from our lives and mix them thoroughly with His "resin" until every piece is immersed in it. Then He can begin the process of creating works of art that bring glory and praise to Him.

What's the "resin" God uses to create something new? It's His Holy Spirit. As He fills us with His Spirit and we submit to His will, He's able to knead us until we're one with His Spirit and ready for His handiwork to be completed in our lives. This process brings healing to all the wounds caused by our parents' efforts or our own efforts to shape the original material.

IT'S NEVER TOO LATE

It's never too late to seek your parents' blessing or to give the blessing to your adult children.

It's never too late to seek your parents' blessing or to give the blessing to your adult children. If you've never asked for your parents' blessing or never given one to your own children before, start today.

You may need to clear away a mound of garbage first—some things your parents dropped on you or you dropped on your children a long time ago, that no one ever bothered to pick up. If so, pick it up now. Go back to those parents or those kids and make it right. Ask them to forgive you for all the times you stumbled. Be specific. You know what those areas are that keep you from the kind of relationship you want with them.

Hurts and wounds can be healed. The resentment can be replaced by an attitude reflecting God's character. The heart of bitterness that destroys a life can become a heart of praise and gratefulness to God.

You may feel that things are beyond saving. You might be thinking, *I really would like to do what you say, Rolf, but I know my kids (or my parents) wouldn't receive it. I know my spouse would laugh at me.* I doubt that anyone would laugh at you, especially if you have truly forgiven them in your heart.

In any case, once you've sought and granted forgiveness, you cannot control their response. You can only control your own.

The most important part is for you to understand that God has forgiven you, and that you only need to draw on that forgiveness. Then you must also forgive yourself. As you walk in the light of that forgiveness, you'll radiate it to those around you. When they see it, they'll be drawn to it. And at that point they can receive your forgiveness and begin to be made whole as well.

In 1974, when Mary and I were still in Puerto Rico, I was asked by my pastor to be one of seven laymen to speak at the Good Friday service in our church. He said that each of us would have five minutes to speak on one of the "seven last words" of Christ on the cross. (Matt. 27:46; Luke 23:34,43,46; John 19:26-30.) When I asked him which of the seven words I was to speak on, he said, "You can take your pick. You're the first person I've asked." I scanned the list and selected the passage from Luke 23:34 KJV: "Father, forgive them; for they know not what they do."

I had more than enough time to prepare for a five-minute talk. *Anyone can talk on forgiveness for five minutes,* I reasoned, so I didn't bother to think about it until the night before I was to speak. As I sat at my desk to scratch out a brief outline, nothing came.

I sat there for several hours reading and rereading the story of the Crucifixion and commentaries on the subject. It was as though my mind had a lid on it. Nothing was coming. I finally gave it a rest.

Early the next morning, I returned to my office looking for some clarity in my thoughts. Nothing. I went to church early, thinking that maybe the surroundings and music might help. Finally, I looked at the bulletin, hoping to see my name at the bottom of the list so I could gain some insight from the other speakers.

Much to my chagrin, I was first on the program. I wondered, *Why am I first? Is it because he asked me first?* And then I saw it! I was first on the program because "Father, forgive them, for they know not what they do" was the first thing Jesus said from the cross. Before He said, "My God, my God, why hast thou forsaken me?" He declared to all around Him—persecutors, friends, families, the curious—"Father, forgive them; they don't know what they're doing." Before He said, "I thirst," He said, "Father, forgive them."

When I realized that Jesus' first concern was the forgiveness of those who were abusing Him, I couldn't wait to speak. No way was five minutes enough to share what I had just discovered.

By His example, Jesus showed us what He would do in and through us when we give Him the opportunity.

By His example, Jesus showed us what He would do in and through us when we give Him the opportunity. The same Spirit that not only allowed Jesus to exhibit this forgiveness, but also raised Him from the dead, is the very Spirit that God wants to fill us with so we can be conformed to His likeness. Then, and only then, can we truly know the power of forgiveness to set us and our offenders free from our past.

Experiencing God's forgiveness liberates us to begin to bless our families instead of cursing them. It opens the door to speak honestly to them without shame or guilt, because Jesus bore our shame and guilt on the cross.

If you're an adult who has never been blessed by your parents, go to them and request it. This will liberate both you and them to experience a new level of love and acceptance. If you're a parent of grown children, go to them and clear up the past. Then ask them to let you bless them. As you do, God will bless you all.

MAY OUR LORD JESUS CHRIST HIMSELF AND *God our Father, who loved us and by his grace gave us eternal encouragement and good hope, encourage your hearts and strengthen you in every good deed and word.*

May the Lord direct your hearts into God's love and Christ's perseverance.

Now may the Lord of peace himself give you peace at all times and in every way.

The Lord be with all of you.

2 THESSALONIANS 2:16,17; 3:5,16 NIV

CHAPTER EIGHT

EXPANDING THE CIRCLE

What about all those "OPKs" ("Other People's Kids") out there? Who will bless them? Someone once said that we may be the only Bible some people ever read. We may also be the only one ever to speak a blessing on some people. Do we dare pass up the opportunity?

Blessing children as defined in this book is not limited to our own children. It's not even limited to children. It extends to include the entire "human family."

Jesus' own example was one of blessing other people's kids. It was typical of Jesus to take the children in His arms, place His hands on them, and bless them. (Mark 10:16.) No doubt kids often surrounded Him—not only because they felt comfortable being near Him, but also because they knew He had a blessing in store for them.

We may be the only Bible some people ever read.

Grandparents are the most obvious folks who are in a position to bless children. They will probably have frequent opportunities to bless their children's children.

My grandfather was a classic example of a blesser. He loved kids; he had fourteen children and twenty-eight grandchildren. We always loved to be with Grandpa. He was continually doing something to make us laugh. And best of all, when we were gathered in the living room, Grandpa would reach in his pocket, jingle his change, and start tossing coins on the carpet. We would all dive into a pile to get our share. It was a kind and loving "blessing" to demonstrate his delight in the little ones around him. Each child knew he had Grandpa's approval, which was important to him.

Instead of dispensing coins to his grandchildren, my dad always carried in his shirt pocket "kokky"—broken pieces of hard candy. Before his grandkids could walk or talk, they understood that Grandpa had "kokky." They knew where to find it and that Grandpa had an unlimited supply. They simply had to crawl up on his lap and dig in.

A relationship with grandparents is extremely important in the self-esteem and character development of a child. Studies suggest that children who have been raised near their grandparents and spend time with them have a heightened sense of security and well-being. Recently I heard of a program to involve grandparents in the lives of children of single mothers. Research by the group sponsoring this program concurred with other studies concerning the value of the presence of a grandfather in the life of a young boy raised by a single mom. This was especially evident for boys age ten to fifteen. If the presence and social involvement of a grandparent can positively impact children in such environments, consider the benefits those children receive when that grandparent actively

A relationship with grandparents is extremely important in the self-esteem and character development of a child.

blesses them. That blessing can include both a verbal, hands-on-the-head, straight-out-of-Numbers 6:24-26 blessing as well as other simple blessings: the spoken words "God bless you," a loving caress, a kind word, an encouraging smile, an understanding nod, a listening ear, a forgiving kiss, a comforting shoulder. All these are accepting and approving signs of interest in the child.

Grandparents often have two important qualities: time and patience.

Grandparents often have two important qualities to contribute in building relationships with children: time and patience. So it's wonderful when they choose to invest that precious commodity in their grandchildren.

My grandmother had a rare quality that was a great blessing for youngsters: serenity. She had the ability to take whatever life brought her with grace, to praise God in both good and bad times, to remain faithful during times of struggle, and to serve others cheerfully without complaining, even when their needs might not have been as great as her own. She certainly earned the title of saint if anyone ever did.

"Gramma," as we called her, came from Norway as a teenager and settled in Superior, Wisconsin. She married Lars Roholt and gave birth to her first seven children at home over a ten-year period. During one four-year stretch of terrible grief, the first, fourth, and sixth-born children (all boys) died: one of scarlet fever at age six, one of typhoid fever at age three, and the last of dehydration at the age of six months. In addition, each of the other four children also nearly died of scarlet fever.

When the sixth child was born, Gramma was so severely crippled with a form of arthritis that she could not comb her own hair for the pain and had to crawl to climb stairs. Yet no one ever heard her complain. She gave her grief to God.

Gramma's arthritis improved significantly when she and her family moved away from the cold and damp conditions around Lake Superior. She soon became a leader in her church. She was a blessing to everyone she met. She also gave birth to seven more children!

By the time she reached her early fifties, Gramma's arthritis returned. For the remainder of her life, she was in constant pain. Yet the most negative remark I ever heard her say regarding her condition was that it kept her from doing more for others. She said, in her thick Norwegian accent, "If I yust had two good legs, I vould run and yump like a spring shicken."

One day when Gramma was ninety-two years old and living with my parents, she hobbled out from her bedroom on her walker and said to my mother, "Ya, Blanche. You know, I vas reading in dis magazine, and I found a vord dat tells yust da type of person dat I am." The word was *optimist.*

She was that all right, and much more. She was also an overcomer, one who considered the needs of others greater than her own and was always looking for ways to share the victory she knew so well in Jesus. She was a "blesser" in every way.

No parent, or even two parents, can meet the constant needs of a child all the time.

Grandparents have a multitude of opportunities to bless grandchildren. A grandparent's role in children's lives is vital. Grandparents often have the time and character qualities that children need.

No parent, or even two parents, can meet the constant needs of a child all the time. So finding other supportive adults to enrich your child's life can provide blessings to both of you. The need to be blessed with a parent's regular attention, approval, and goodwill is real and extremely difficult to fill consistently by most parents.

Caring adult Christians can become "blessing activists." Look for those to whom you can give a thoughtful, encouraging word. The world is full of opportunities to give a sincere, loving compliment, to say a word to brighten a child's day, or to show them that you care.

It doesn't take much time to express a blessing or two on a daily basis. Just consider the places you go where you could encounter an opportunity to bless a child. Ask God to show you what you can do to start blessing those "OPKs."

The biblical gift of blessing was not limited to blessing children; people of *all* ages should receive the favor and power of God. We all have a child within. If that child was never blessed, it's still looking for the blessing. The search doesn't end when we become adults.

It may be a brother or sister who needs a blessing, or perhaps a friend or coworker.

Most of us have a number of close contacts with adults outside our family whose ongoing relationships could provide the opportunity for speaking a blessing.

Countless people, whether children or adults, are waiting for someone to speak God's blessing into their lives. The possibilities for blessing are endless. Start today.

NOW TO HIM WHO IS ABLE TO KEEP YOU *from stumbling, and to make you stand in the presence of His glory blameless with great joy, to the only God our Savior, through Jesus Christ our Lord, be glory, majesty, dominion and authority, before all time and now and forever. Amen.*

JUDE 24,25 NAS

CHAPTER NINE

BLESSING AS A WAY OF LIFE

And give you peace.

Everybody loved my father—everybody, that is, except Mr. and Mrs. Aune. They were neighbors on the lake where we lived for thirteen years. It wasn't a personal thing. At least it didn't start out that way.

Twenty years before we moved into the house next to theirs, the Aunes had a severe crossing of wills with a member of their church. Rather than resolve that conflict, they became extremely bitter—not just toward that other member or even the entire membership of their church. No, they were bitter toward anyone who attended church anywhere. And they told anyone who would listen.

The Aunes were in their mid-sixties when we met. When they learned that we were Christians, they wanted nothing to do with our faith or us. We tried to honor their wishes. But God had other plans.

Our home was on a lake on several acres of land, giving our dog Shultz ample room to run. But somehow it was never enough, so he often visited the Aunes' yard as well. Shultz's trespassing especially bothered Mrs. Aune. She showed her frustration by shouting various things at him, none of which he understood. She even notified the town constable about Shultz. We tried to keep Shultz home, but when a boat pulling a water skier came close to our shoreline, a ball and chain could not have held him.

The day finally came when Mrs. Aune and Shultz had a showdown. She was out in her yard digging dandelions, using a picker with a five-foot wooden handle on one end and a sharp, twin-pointed blade on the other. When Shultz came flying through her yard, she wound up like a baseball pitcher and let the lethal weapon fly.

She wound up like a baseball pitcher and let the lethal weapon fly.

Fortunately for Shultz, she was out of practice and the lance sailed harmlessly over his back.

Within minutes, Mrs. Aune was pounding on our door. Having observed the encounter through our windows, my dad offered to greet our visitor.

The next few moments I'll never forget. As my dad opened the door, there was Mrs. Aune, literally bouncing up and down with rage, like some plastic wind-up toy.

For what seemed like eternity, Mrs. Aune screamed at my dad at the top of her lungs. When she ran out of words, she stood there sputtering like an old motor. Finally, she ran out of gas and stopped. With his heart overflowing with compassion, my father replied, "My dear Mrs. Aune, I am so sorry that we have upset you so. Will you ever forgive us? We'll try not to let it happen again. God bless you, Mrs. Aune." For a brief moment, she stood there in stunned silence. She was defenseless. Then she spun on her heels and charged back across the yard.

For several weeks we didn't see Mr. and Mrs. Aune, and Dad became concerned. Their lawn, usually nicely kept, was overgrown and in desperate need of mowing. So after considerable prodding from Dad, my brother and I were finally convinced to mow their lawn. We were about fourteen and sixteen years old at the time, and this wasn't how we had planned to spend a warm summer day at the lake. It was an all-day job to mow and rake their large lawn. But we did it, however reluctantly.

No sign of life appeared in the Aune house while we worked, but we knew they were home. Two weeks later, my brother and I again protested as Dad asked us to mow their lawn. This time we saw Mrs. Aune peeking from behind the curtains.

Two more weeks passed when Dad looked over at the Aunes' lawn and said, "Well, boys?" We knew what that meant. This time just as we were finishing, Mrs. Aune came outside carrying a tray with a large glass of lemonade for each of us. She thanked us for mowing her lawn and explained that her husband, Al, had not been well. We told her we were sorry and were glad to help in any way we could. Later that fall, Mrs Aune called. "Can you come quickly? A1 is very ill." Mom and Dad rushed to their home. Mrs. Aune took them to the bedroom where her husband lay. They talked with Mr. Aune about his illness, his past with the church, the state of his soul, and the redeeming blood of Christ that could make him clean again. Mr. Aune listened, thanked them, and asked them to please come back.

Over the next few weeks, Dad and Mom visited the Aunes several times. Finally, the day came when both Mr. and Mrs. Aune prayed to receive Christ as their Savior. I can still remember my parents' joy when they told us the story.

Two weeks later, Mr. Aune went to be with the Lord. Mrs. Aune joined our church, soaking up everything she could. The following summer she was baptized in Lake Wissota. She grew in her faith and became a close friend of our family. Then a few years later she joined her husband. What would have happened to Mr. and Mrs. Aune if my dad had responded to her in a harsh way that summer afternoon? Instead, God used a soft answer, a kind word, a loving deed, a blessing, to expand His kingdom here on earth.

Much of what I've learned about blessing I learned from my father.

Dad's response to Mrs. Aune that day was not an isolated instance of Christlikeness. Much of what I've learned about blessing I learned from my father. He not only was a man who knew how to bless people, he used the blessing as a way of life.

The biblical portrait of King David shows us another man who knew the blessing as a way of life. In fact, of the many recorded uses in the Bible of some form of the word *bless,* more than seventy are attributed to David. And on one particular occasion, when he regained the ark of the Lord from his enemies, this king displayed a pattern that we might all want to imitate. At that time David spoke a blessing in three directions. We read that he blessed God for His goodness, saying, "Blessed be the Lord, the God of Israel, from everlasting even to everlasting" (1 Chron. 16:36 NAS). He also blessed all the people around him: "David finished giving burnt offerings and fellowship offerings [to God]. Then he used the Lord's name to bless the people" (v. 2). Finally, he gave the blessing to his family: "Then all the people left. Each person went to his own home. And David also went home to bless his family" (v. 43).

As we read the many stories about David in Scripture, we read about someone who seems to have been continually blessing God, blessing his family, and blessing the people. His son

Solomon was evidently so impressed with the example that he followed the pattern his father had established. (1 Kings 8:12-15.) No wonder, then, that King David, the man of blessing, was called a man after God's own heart, who would do everything God wanted him to do. (Acts 13:22.)

EXPANDING THE CIRCLE OF INFLUENCE

The family blessing spoken regularly over kids is just the center of a circle of influence that can widen to include our interactions in all relationships. Beginning the process may seem like a daunting challenge. But the beauty of it all is that change begins with the first blessing. A single point of commitment in establishing a habit that takes only minutes provides a lifetime of benefits.

Change begins with the first blessing.

When we start by learning to be faithful in little things, we can go on to become faithful in greater things. (Matt. 25:21.)

Blessing our children and others around us is like so many other disciplines of the Christian life. It can all too easily be swept under the rug and neglected. The problem with our "under-the-rug" tendency is that we soon end up with so much there, both good and bad, that we don't know where to start to clean it all up. That's normal. It happens to all of us. Ultimately, we have to deal with what's under the rug. It's better to start now than to wait until later. It's a lie to think that having garbage in your life is okay as long as you keep it hidden.

Ultimately, we have to deal with what's under the rug.

I once went through a particularly difficult time spiritually. I had so much garbage under the carpets, in the corners, and in every closet of my life that it was starting to spill over into noticeable areas. When things finally got desperate, I cried out to God for help.

He began a wonderful heart cleansing. He walked through every room of my heart, shining the gentle light of His Holy Spirit into each dark corner. There was no condemnation or judgment, just the knowledge that everything was going to be fine.

I asked, "Lord, how will we ever clean this mess up?" And He responded, *Don't worry about that. We'll take it one room at a time.* Then I was reminded of the comfort in Paul's words to the Philippians: "Being confident of this very thing, that he which hath begun a good work in you will perform it until the day of Jesus Christ" (1:6 KJV).

On that particular day when God began this cleansing work in me, an article in the local paper caught my eye. The story was about an old, stately mansion in St. Paul, Minnesota, that had been the pride and joy of its original owners. Through years of rough use and poor maintenance, the home had fallen into disrepair. Finally, it was abandoned and slated to be demolished.

Only days before the scheduled demolition, a young couple drove by and, looking beyond the obvious, saw what it could become. They decided to buy it for restoration. An unusual agreement was finally reached: The city sold them the mansion for one dollar on the condition that they move in on the day of closing. The couple agreed. The house was a filthy, rat-infested, broken-windowed disaster, fit only to be destroyed—to everyone, that is, but the new owners. After a three-year renovation, the home reflected the character of the young couple in every room. When the reporter who initially interviewed them inquired how they managed to tackle this job, they replied that after walking through each room, noting what needed to be done, they decided to finish one room at a time until the task was completed.

I'm deeply grateful that God in His wisdom deals with us that way. We are all a work in progress, being remodeled by His Spirit. That should give us hope for the changes taking place in our lives and the lives of our family members.

We are all a work in progress, being remodeled by His Spirit.

As you've read this book, I pray that God has spoken to you. Perhaps He's made you aware of some lumps in your carpet and offered to help you clean it up.

Let Him start cleaning now. Just as the newly remodeled mansion reflected the character of the couple who bought it, let God begin to reflect His character in your life through His remodeling efforts.

Maybe some of *The Family Blessing* rings true, while other points don't relate to your experience at all. That's as it should be. It's like going through a smörgåsbord: More than likely everything tastes good, but not all of it appeals to you at once. So take what you can benefit from now and begin to put it to work in your life.

Start with the part that is most important to you. Perhaps you need restoration with the parents who never blessed you. Maybe your concern is forgiveness from your children who are grown and gone. Maybe God is emphasizing to you to speak well of others. Whatever it is, start there.

It's not important to understand everything before you do anything. Begin to apply the principles of blessing by starting *where you are.* Apply what you do understand and make some mistakes along the way rather than wait until everything is clear. It will all become clear in time.

Meanwhile, in the beginning, don't be afraid of "botching things up." Others will be supportive and eager to help. If your heart is right in what you do, God will make up the difference.

Start to bless today! The blessing carries with it rich rewards that begin to accrue immediately. The apostle Paul said, "The Lord has assigned to each his task. I planted the seed, Apollos watered it, but God made it grow . . . and each will be rewarded according to his own labor" (1 Cor. 3:5-6,8 NIV). God has assigned to each of us the task of blessing others, and He will give the reward.

The blessing carries with it rich rewards that begin to accrue immediately.

Perhaps the greatest reward of blessing is the heritage it allows us to leave our children—the kind of heritage my father left for my brothers and me.

Dad was a giant in my eyes. He was a hard worker and a good provider. And he showed his love for my mother and his boys.

Every greeting to us included a hug and an "I love you." He never raised his voice to my mother, and I never heard them argue or fight.

As a child, every morning as I stumbled out of my bedroom, I would see Dad lying on the couch reading his

Bible and praying. His one overwhelming motivation in life was to see his three boys come to know and love God with all their hearts.

Dad and Mom prayed together daily. Their prayers included the request that each son would find a wife who loved him and shared his faith and commitment to the Lord. Those prayers have been wonderfully answered.

When Mary and I were married, we received many beautiful gifts and loving wishes. One gift in particular that we treasure to this day was the Scripture verse my parents gave us as a lifelong blessing on our marriage: "And be ye kind one to another, tenderhearted, forgiving one another, even as God for Christ's sake hath forgiven you" (Eph. 4:32 KJV).

Dad kept short accounts, whether it was in business or in personal relationships. One of my favorite stories he used to tell us as kids concerned the little girl in Norway who asked her mother when Jesus was coming back.

"Well," her mother told her, "we don't know when that will be. It could be at any time."

The daughter thought for a moment and said, "Then, Mother, it's pretty important that we have our suitcase packed, isn't it?"

Dad's bags were always packed. He was always ready to go.

On a cold January morning in 1985, Mom and Dad rose early, well before dawn as always, and went to their favorite chairs to read and pray together. Besides the Bible, Dad's favorite book was a devotional by the Norwegian author Frederick Wisloff called *Rest a While.* He had read it through countless times in both Norwegian and English. Following is the passage he read that morning:

> *Like a weaver I have rolled up my life; He cuts me off from the loom; from day to night Thou dost bring me to an end.*
>
> ISAIAH 38:12

> A human life is likened unto a tapestry that is to be woven. Day by day the shuttle moves back and forth, and the tapestry grows. As thread is laid upon thread, the design begins to emerge. A thread is such a tiny thing. And yet the whole tapestry is made

> up of such threads. If some threads are improperly woven, the whole design will be marred.
>
> A day appears so small and insignificant. And yet, each day is a part of my whole life. If each single day is lived improperly and carelessly, what will this do to the design of my life?
>
> When the tapestry is finished, it is rolled up, and the ends of the threads are cut off. Then it can be woven no more. It is put away until the day when it is placed on exhibition and judged.
>
> Dear God, grant that the tapestry of my life may be properly woven. I give Thee the shuttle. Do with me as Thou wilt, if only Thy image may some day be the design in my tapestry when the threads of my life are cut off, and the tapestry is judged.[1]

When Dad finished reading this, he wept as he poured out his heart to his Father in prayer. Dad rarely cried—except in prayer. When he prayed, he was often so overwhelmed by God's love that he would weep with gratitude. This day he was as grateful as ever for all that God had done.

As he prayed, Dad interceded, as always, for his wife, his boys, and their families. He then prayed for himself, that an improperly woven thread would not mar the tapestry of his life. He prayed that God would cleanse him of all areas of sin in his life, and that he would be clean as he stood before Him.

That evening my brother and his wife ate supper with my parents. As they sat around the table afterward, Dad said, "You know, I have been dreaming a lot lately, and it is usually the same dream. I see myself as part of a vast multitude of believers standing before the throne of God, and we are all worshiping the Lord. Sometimes I look around at the people, and I recognize some as friends. I then realize that all of these friends have died. Do you think there is anything to these dreams?"

My brother and his wife didn't quite know what to say. Two days earlier, Dad had given a friend a hug and said to him, "You know, Terry, I just long to be with my Lord, don't you?" So they wondered about what all this might mean.

Later that evening, after a bowl of ice cream and the evening news, Dad gave Mom a tender hug, told her how much he loved her, breathed out a sigh, and was gone—gone to be with the Lord he loved and served. He was seventy-eight.

Not a day goes by without a reminder of Dad. For instance, when my son was going through some times of searching and questioning his faith, I felt I should visit him at college. As we talked well into the night, he reminisced.

Not a day goes by without a reminder of Dad.

"Dad," he recalled, "four years ago when Grandpa was alive, I stopped by to see him and Grandma. We talked for a while, and as I was about to leave, I gave them both a hug and a kiss and told them I loved them. Then Grandpa said, 'Carlton, you know, my deepest desire for you is that you know and love the Lord with all your heart.'

"You know, Dad," Carlton said, "those are the last words Grandpa ever said to me." We both cried.

Several weeks after Dad went to be with the Lord, Mom was going through his belongings. Tucked away was a letter to his three sons and our families. It was written in his own hand, and it reminisced about his childhood in Norway, meeting our mother, and his love for the Lord. Before the letter ended, he made certain we knew what was beating most in his heart for us:

> *Now in closing I just want you to know that we love you all—children, your spouses, grandchildren, and great-grandchildren. We pray for you and mention your name before the throne of grace every day. Our most sincere prayer is that we may all meet home in that glory land someday. Stay close to Jesus, and He will stay close to you. Jesus says, "Fear not, for I am with you. Be not dismayed for I am your God, I will help you and strengthen you and uphold you with the right hand of my righteousness."*

In these words, Dad gave us his blessing. In a powerful sense his whole *life* was a blessing. He knew the heart of God, and he desired that his three boys and their families would also know the heart of God. To that end he committed his life—a commitment that my mother shared and carries on with her through prayers and blessings.

The family blessing is an active commitment to our children's highest good.

What is the family blessing? It's an active commitment to our children's highest good, that they might know and love the Lord their God with all their hearts.

Perhaps the story of my father's last day can help us consider the big picture of our lives. Each little word, each interaction with our kids is a thread that joins many others to form the fabric of our children's character. What will that fabric be? Each attitude we cultivate is a stitch in the tapestry of our own lives. What will be the final pattern of that tapestry when we one day present it to God for His approval? If we learn, as my father did, to make the blessing a way of life, our children's fabric will be strong. The tapestry of a godly example we leave as their heritage will be beautiful. Then truly the Lord will bless us and keep us; the Lord will make His face to shine upon us and be gracious to us; the Lord will lift up His countenance upon us and give us peace. For what greater blessing could we ask?

START PRACTICING THE FAMILY BLESSING

1. Now is the time to start blessing your children. It's never too early for them to begin receiving the benefits of being blessed. Read this book through once a month or until the message of blessing becomes a personal passion in your life. Take full advantage of the time you have—start today!
2. Find a consistent time to bless your family. There are no right or wrong times or frequencies—simply pray and seek God about what is best for your family. Remember, structure and consistency are important, especially to young children.
3. Seek God's wisdom on what biblical or biblically-inspired blessing is right for your family and begin to use it. Remember, all the blessings don't have to be the same every time.
4. Explain to your children what a blessing is and why you are speaking it over them. Remember, use meaningful touch (a hug, hand on a shoulder, etc.) when blessing them.
5. Supplement the blessing with a prayer over your children and expect to see amazing results!
6. Share with others the rewards of blessing. Explain to aunts, uncles, grandparents, and friends what you are doing and encourage them to practice the blessing in their own lives. Encourage them to either use the blessings provided in *The Family Blessing,* or establish their own biblically inspired blessing.
7. Tell your pastor what you are doing and ask him or her to pray for you as you begin.
8. Look for opportunities to bless others (neighbors, coworkers, friends, etc.). Adapt a lifestyle of blessing.
9. Share how practicing *The Family Blessing* has changed your life. Send your inspirational stories to:

familyblessingrg@aol.com

— or —

Rolf Garborg
4090 154th Street
Prior Lake, MN 55372

ENDNOTES

Chapter 1

[1] Larry Christensen, *The Christian Family* (Minneapolis: Bethany Fellowship, 1970). The section of this excellent book that first introduced me to the notion of the family blessing is on pages 195-197, "Presenting Your Children to God Through Blessing."

[2] Author's adaptation of the text from the *King James Version.*

Chapter 2

[1] Larry G. Lenning, *Blessing in Mosque and Mission* (Pasadena, California: William Carey Library, 1980), p. 74. Much of the material in this chapter was drawn from this excellent study of the notion of blessing.

[2] John R. Kohlenberger III and James A. Swanson, *New International Version Exhaustive Concordance,* 2nd ed. (Grand Rapids: Zondervan, 1999).

Chapter 3

[1] From *Fiddler on the Roof* by Jerry Bock, Sheldon Harnick, and Arnold Perl. Music and lyrics copyright © 1964 by Sunbeam Music Corp. Used with permission.

Chapter 4

[1] Zig Ziglar, *See You at the Top* (Gretna, Louisiana: Pelican Publishing Company, Inc. Copyright © 1975, 1977 by Zig Ziglar) pp. 118-119.

Chapter 5

[1] Gary Smalley & John Trent, *The Blessing* (Nashville, Tennessee: Thomas Nelson, 1986) p. 61.

Chapter 7

[1] Lenning, pp. 94-95.

Chapter 9

[1] Frederick Wisloff, *Rest a While.* This cherished devotional, worn out by my father in both English and Norwegian, was originally published in Norwegian in 1948 under the title, *Hvil Eder Litt,* by Indremisjonsforlaget A.S., Oslo, Norway.

ABOUT THE AUTHOR

Rolf Garborg began his thirty-five-year ministry in the Christian Publishing industry as a twenty-two-year-old missionary in Puerto Rico selling books door to door. That meager beginning evolved into the establishment of a successful Christian bookstore and distribution center on the island, as well as the founding of Editorial Betania, a Spanish publishing house that continues today.

Upon returning to the United States in 1975, Rolf continued in leadership for a variety of publishing organizations before co-founding Garborg's, a Christian gift company. Since Garborg's was sold in 2001, he has begun Garborg & Associates, a consulting company serving the Christian publishing and gift industries. Rolf's career has taken him to all fifty states and over eighty countries, providing him the opportunity to bless and be blessed the world over.

Rolf has been married for more than thirty years to Mary. They are blessed with two children and three grandchildren. Rolf and Mary currently reside in Minnesota.

Additional copies of *The Family Blessing*
and other titles by Rolf Garborg
are available from your local bookstore.

Visit our website at:
www.whitestone books.com